Wolves

PHOTOS AND FACTS FOR EVERYONE

BY ISIS GAILLARD

Learn With Facts Series

Book 74

Dedicated to my boys Jaxon and Jalen
_____

CONTENTS

Introduction	6
Description	9
Size	12
Breeding	13
Eating Habit	16
Interesting Facts	18

Copyright ©2022 by Isis Gaillard All rights reserved. No part of this book may be used or reproduced in any manner whatsoever without the express written permission of the publisher except for the use of brief quotations in a book review

The author and publisher make no warranty, expressed or implied, that the information contained herein is appropriate for all individuals, situations or purposes, and assume no responsibility for errors or omission. The reader assumes the risk and full responsibility for all actions, and the authors will not be held liable for any loss or damage, whether consequential.

Image Credits: Royalty-free images reproduced under license from various stock image repositories.

Isis Gaillard. Wolves: Photos and Fun Facts for Kids (Kids Learn With Pictures Series Book 83). Ebook Edition.
Learn With Facts an imprint of TLM Media LLC

eISBN: 978-1-63497-200-0
ISBN-13: 978-1-63497-327-4

Introduction

The gray wolf is the largest member of the species canid, which refers to all dog type animals. Wolves average 80 to 100 pounds, with females being smaller than males. They look very similar to the German Shepard but with larger heads, longer legs, and bigger paws.

The wolf's hair coat may be a mottled gray color or pure white. Wolves have even been seen with red, brown, and black hair coats. The wolf's jaw is extremely strong with heavy, large teeth that are best suited to crushing bones, unlike the domestic dog.

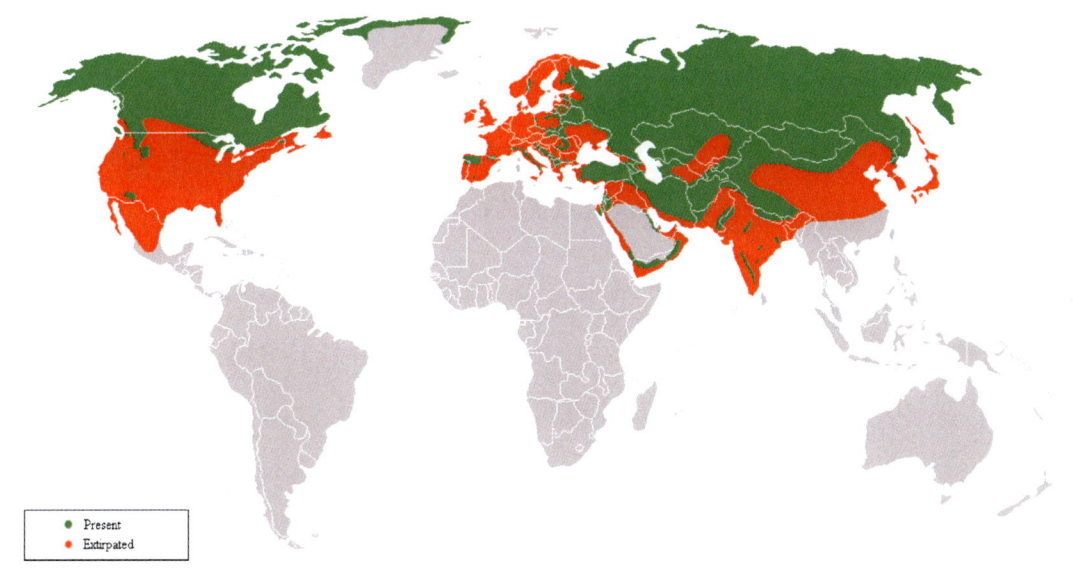

The Gray Wolf is a native to the wilderness. In North America, the wolf once dominated the rocky mountain region of Alaska, Canada, and the northern states. Although the wolf was almost hunted to extinction by cattle ranchers, recent efforts to reintroduce the wolf to these areas have seen great success. In Eurasia, the wolf roams similar wilderness and mountainous regions of Russia, Mongolia, China, and certain parts of Europe. These habitats have an abundance of the large game, which makes up the wolf's dietary preference. In contrast, wolves have been confirmed to inhabit some African countries like Ethiopia, Algeria, and Senegal. Likewise, in North America, the wolf also populates the more arid regions of Arizona and New Mexico.

Description

Believed to be the origin of the **wolf** species is the African wolf native to North and East Africa. From the Indian subcontinent, we get the Himalayan wolf coming from Kashmir, Tibet, and Nepal. The youngest subspecies of the wolf are now the most predominant species known as the European and North American Gray Wolf. Of these, we have the Eurasian wolf, which has the largest range of all wolf species. The Mexican wolf roams northern Mexico and southern Texas and tends to be smaller than their cousins. The Northern Rocky Mountains wolf, on the other hand, tends to be the largest of all subspecies.

Wolves are highly gregarious animals meaning that they are social and form packs in which they live. Usually, a pack will consist of a single pair, male and female, that will mate during their lifespans. This pair will ideally produce a litter of 3 to 6 pups every year. These pups will stay with the pack for as long as four years before dispersing to form their packs. Because of this longevity and the mating pair, the pack will be comprised of several juveniles that have yet to reach sexual maturity and several yearlings. Packs may grow as large as 11 members before the juveniles start to leave

Wolf packs are extremely territorial. They will establish a territory by scent marking through urination, defecation, and ground scratching at various intervals around the perimeter of their area. If other wolves breach this perimeter, the pack will fiercely defend their territory through direct attacks. Wolves are also very vocal communicators when it comes to territorial protection. However, during times when their preferred food sources are abundant, such as in large migrations of elk, different packs have been known to join forces. Also, packs rarely adopt a lone wolf unless it is an immature juvenile or if one of the adults in the mating pair has died and a replacement from outside the pack is required.

Size

Males average 5 to 6.5 feet in length from nose to tip of tail. Females average 4.5 to 6 feet. Most wolves stand at 26 to 32 inches at the shoulder. Females weight 60 to 80 pounds. Males weight 70 to 110 pounds.

A wolf footprint will measure 4 inches wide by 5 inches long

Breeding

Wolves are typically monogamous, mating with the same partner throughout their lifespan. Only mature males that do not have a mate will attempt to breed with females from other established packs. Females are capable of producing more than one litter per year but ideally only want to support one litter each year. Breeding season occurs during the late winter, and the gestation period is around 2 ½ months. Therefore, litters are born in late Spring to early Summer when food sources are becoming more abundant.

Wolf pups are born blind and deaf with the instinct to nurse from their mothers who will not leave the den where they are born for the first few weeks. It is up to the fathers to bring food to the den for the mother while she is constantly nursing her pups. After about ten days, the pups' eyes begin opening. They will greatly increase in size and first be able to leave the den at around three weeks of age.

Wolves Photos and Facts For Everyone | Page 13

Within a month to six weeks, pups can eat solid food and flee from danger. As with all canids, wolf pups play fight from the time they begin leaving the den. These play fights escalate as the pups mature to establish dominance between siblings and build a hierarchy. By the time these pups are 5 to 6 months old, they will accompany the adults on hunts and begin learning how to catch and kill prey.

Eating Habit

Wolves are largely carnivores, meaning they eat meat and have a wide variety of choices to satisfy their diet. Within wilderness areas, wolf packs will hunt moose, deer, elk, wild boar, bighorn sheep, and even bison. While they prefer the abundance of food gained from these large animals, wolves will hunt rabbits, badgers, foxes, squirrels, beavers, and other rodents to supplement their dietary needs. Within areas inhabited by humans, wolves become more opportunistic by preying on livestock like cattle, sheep, pigs, and chickens. Wolves are even known to scavenge garbage from people's homes and landfills.

Eating Habit

In times where food sources are scarce such during harsh winters, wolf packs will attack weak or injured wolves, whether from rival packs or within their own. The wolf will also feed carcasses of dead wolves. In addition to meat, wolves will readily consume berries, nightshades, apples, pears, melons, and other naturally growing vegetation to fulfill their daily nutritional requirements.

Interesting Facts

1. Wolves are the largest members of the Canidae family.
2. Wolves can live up to 13 years in the wild.
3. Wolves have 42 teeth.
4. They have four toes with claws in an oval shape. They run on their toes, not their pads.
5. Wolves mate for life.
6. A litter of wolves is usually 4 to 6 pups.
7. Pups are born deaf and blind with bright blue eyes.
8. A pack of wolves can range from 2 to over 30 wolves. On average they run in packs between 5 and 8 wolves.
9. Wolves can run at 36 to 38 MPH.
10. Wolves were killed off in Montana in the late 1930's, but were reintroduced in Yellowstone National Park the 1995 and 1996 and their numbers are currently increasing.
11. In 2013, there were at least 625 wolves in western Montana.
12. The Montana Fish, Wildlife, and Parks allows up to 100 wolves to be hunted per year.
13. Gray wolves can range in color from gray, black, tan, or white.

THE END

Thanks for reading facts about Wolves. I am a parent of two boys on the autism spectrum. I am always advocating for Autism Spectrum Disorders which part of the proceeds of this book goes to many Non-Profit Autism Organizations. I would love if you would leave a review.

Author Note from Isis Gaillard:

Thanks For Reading! I hope you enjoyed the fact book about Wolves.

Please check out all the Learn With Facts and the Kids Learn With Pictures series available.

Visit www.IsisGaillard.com and www.LearnWithFacts.com to find more books in the **Learn With Facts Series**

More Books In The Series

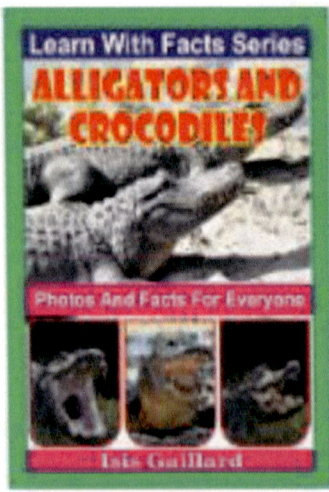  

Over 75 books in the Learn With Facts Series.

Set 1

```
A L L X R F K Y S A S I X K P
S Q H Y N O W O G R B G S O W
E L X D B X O B A I A D O R R
L G W B Z E U Y T L R G F R D
E K G O O S B X Z I A V U U F
P L D W H I E H B E I S Y O S
H S D V I C E C T E Y W C H C
A C H I N C H I L L A S A I J
N S S B N N F A F J L T Y A L
T O E U T O F P M V E D C I S
S O D S M F S V T E R S O W R
E R Z O R A G A H Y L N Q V A
A A F E L O T C U I S E Q Y E
G G Q R G P H O K R A K O L B
L N T C X X H Z P F S E A N B
E A L I S E L I D O C O R C S
S K D E K V W S N D P N D Z I
S G O H E G D E H S O P F G I
F H S R E V A E B P C C I B S
A H B P E G I R A F F E S H E
```

Word List

Bears
Beavers
Birds
Chameleons
Cheetahs
Chinchillas
Cougars
Crocodiles
Dinosaurs

Dolphins
Eagles
Elephants
Foxes
Frogs
Giraffes
Hedgehogs
Hippopotamus
Horses

Kangaroos
Koalas
Lions
Owls

Set 2

Z	G	K	M	V	B	E	E	S	S	O	V	E	E	P
P	E	A	C	O	C	K	S	F	R	A	N	E	Y	H
G	I	P	Z	A	L	L	I	G	A	T	O	R	S	B
C	J	G	A	E	N	F	V	S	U	U	L	Y	C	R
Y	R	R	U	N	L	X	Z	R	G	Q	K	C	S	C
H	S	I	F	A	D	L	Y	E	A	N	O	E	I	K
R	P	C	D	H	N	A	E	G	J	T	I	P	H	S
H	I	F	A	N	W	A	S	I	X	P	O	X	N	S
I	D	Z	A	M	A	P	S	T	P	Q	I	E	A	Y
N	E	F	L	H	E	S	B	U	X	T	T	R	G	H
O	R	L	P	G	M	L	P	T	O	T	B	B	S	S
C	S	A	A	U	M	D	S	A	I	E	A	L	E	I
E	A	M	C	E	N	W	S	K	Z	T	C	R	A	F
R	A	I	A	A	U	N	D	M	S	R	T	W	T	Y
O	L	N	S	S	I	N	K	S	E	F	F	V	U	L
S	J	G	Z	U	A	V	E	N	R	R	T	K	R	L
G	O	O	G	S	O	C	B	A	H	S	I	A	T	E
D	I	N	T	F	C	B	Y	K	Q	Z	C	B	L	J
B	E	A	Q	B	U	T	T	E	R	F	L	I	E	S
P	C	I	N	S	E	C	T	S	E	V	Q	K	S	Z

Word List

Alligators	Flamingo	Penguins
Alpacas	Gazelle	Rhinoceros
Bats	Hyena	Sea Turtles
Bees	Iguanas	Snakes
Butterflies	Insects	Spiders
Camels	Jaguars	Tigers
Cats and Kittens	Jellyfish	Zebras
Dogs and Puppies	Pandas	
Fish	Peacocks	

Set 3

```
P S G U K P O N I E S C M M S
O A N S O C T O P U S E S I E
T T R O E R O O S T E R S Q A
C S K R I F K K J M Y P W S L
M Y J A O P O V J L C I A G S
W K C Q E T R W E S U G N G A
H Z E F I Y S O R A V S S O N
W O L V E S P A C E S A S S D
L G Y Z W A E S S Y N W T S
V X T L R B D O N D O D N R E
H G I D R R O A Y G S P S I A
W E S A A M C G A T T I E C L
U H L Z X I G R P A A G A H I
L O I E L T D E K B R L H E O
P L O E X O U R I S F E O S N
L N P Q D A E R D G I T R N S
B R P O V E S W T X S S S V S
A E M L M L Y N X L H T E W G
D O O X X O W H A L E S S H M
K V R A N T E A T E R S A J T
```

Word List

Anteater
Komodo Dragons
Leopards
Lizards
Lynx
Meerkat
Moose
Octopuses
Ostriches

Parrots
Pelicans
Pigs and Piglets
Polar Bears
Ponies
Roosters
Scorpions
Seahorses
Seals and Sea Lions

Starfish
Swans
Turtles
Whales
Wolves

Set 4

```
Z P O R C U P I N E S C M F Z
P K N S K C E O Y U H A O A I
E C H I D N A R F M O E U A H
K H C K W Q E E S E R R N K F
R M P L S E U K Y G O A T S X
N A R L D Q R J N E C H A P V
S H C N A O U U G B H P I B L
T Y I C T T P I U B I L N B I
C E E S O F Y F R E C T L Z V
R O G K E O F P Z R K D I S E
F D W I N A N L U R E O O L D
E W I S L O G S L S N L N O N
R E T O V V D X U A S G S T A
R C H I P M U N K S M W W H I
E W S H A R K S D Q S A M S N
T I D Y C Z O O T H O R A D A
S Y T E G U I N E A P I G S M
J S E T E S E E R D L O J T S
J K H H F R P S K U N K S N A
X A R M A D I L L O C E R L T
```

Word List

Armadillo
Buffalo
Chickens
Chipmunks
Cows
Deer
Donkeys
Echidna
Emu

Ferrets
Goats
Guinea Pigs
Llama
Mountain Lions
Platypus
Porcupines
Raccoons
Reindeer

Sharks
Sheep
Skunks
Sloths
Squirrels
Storks
Tasmanian Devil

Set 5

3	W	M	S	E	S	I	O	T	R	O	T	T	X	M
O	Q	M	A	R	S	U	P	I	A	L	S	S	S	V
D	B	G	Z	R	J	A	D	D	G	V	B	C	E	A
A	A	V	V	H	I	S	L	A	M	M	A	M	T	N
N	S	L	A	M	I	N	A	M	R	A	F	S	O	T
G	B	J	B	K	X	S	E	Y	O	X	R	M	Y	E
E	G	A	E	T	U	X	K	L	P	X	I	U	O	L
R	P	U	M	R	N	C	F	S	I	C	C	S	C	O
O	C	U	L	O	A	O	L	R	B	F	T	S	F	P
U	M	A	F	T	J	E	U	S	V	R	E	O	Y	E
S	W	V	T	F	S	I	R	B	A	E	I	P	A	S
A	C	L	M	A	I	U	U	M	D	P	J	O	A	A
N	E	X	E	I	M	N	P	A	N	T	H	E	R	S
I	M	W	G	E	M	H	S	I	T	I	H	B	D	G
M	X	T	L	P	I	Y	F	B	U	L	T	N	V	R
A	J	A	D	B	G	A	S	Q	R	E	B	C	A	L
L	T	D	I	Y	B	K	N	R	K	S	Q	W	R	B
S	P	A	P	V	O	S	O	J	E	S	W	F	K	D
U	N	V	B	N	O	D	L	G	Y	S	J	V	S	Y
S	J	G	O	R	I	L	L	A	S	A	S	A	E	H

Word List

30 Dangerous Animals
Aardvarks
Amphibians
Antelopes
Cattle
Coyotes
Farm Animals
Gorillas
Lemurs
Mammals
Marine Life
Marsupials
Opossums
Panthers
Puffins
Reptiles
Tortoises
Turkeys
Walrus
Weasels
Yaks

Set 1

Set 2

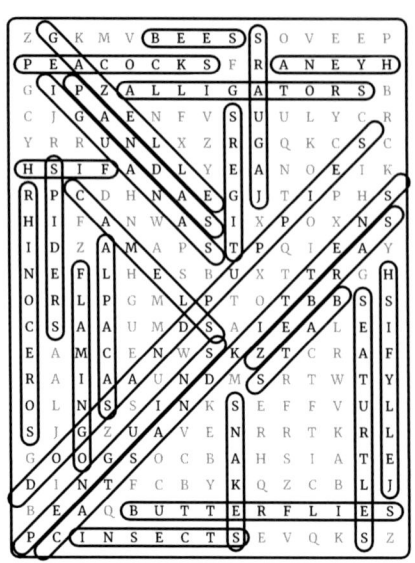

Set 3

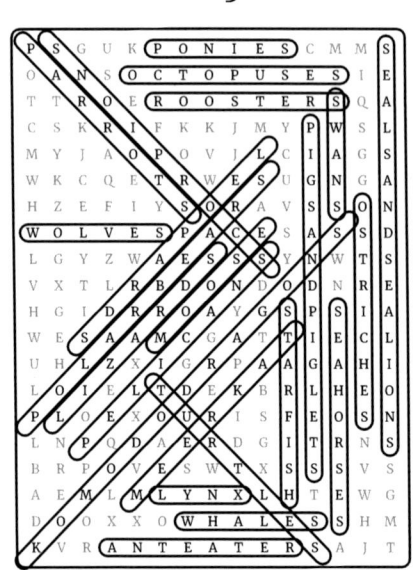

Set 4

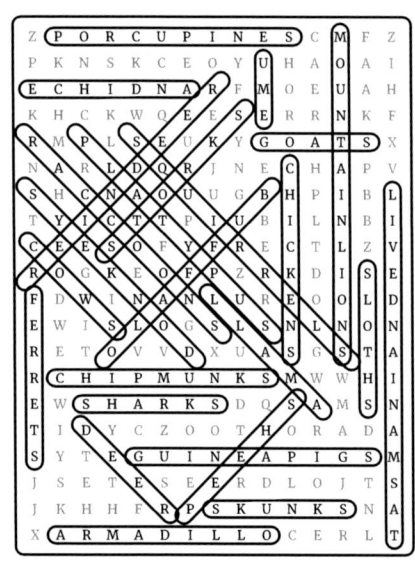

Set 5

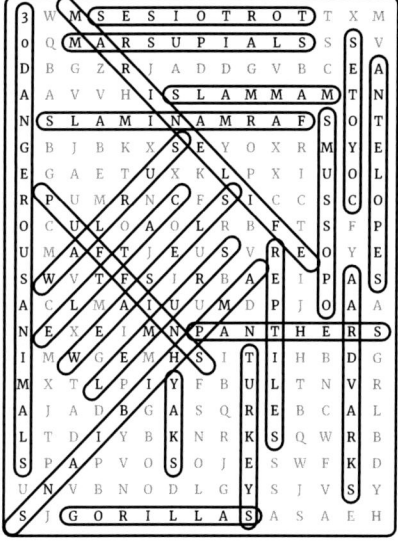

Puzzle 1

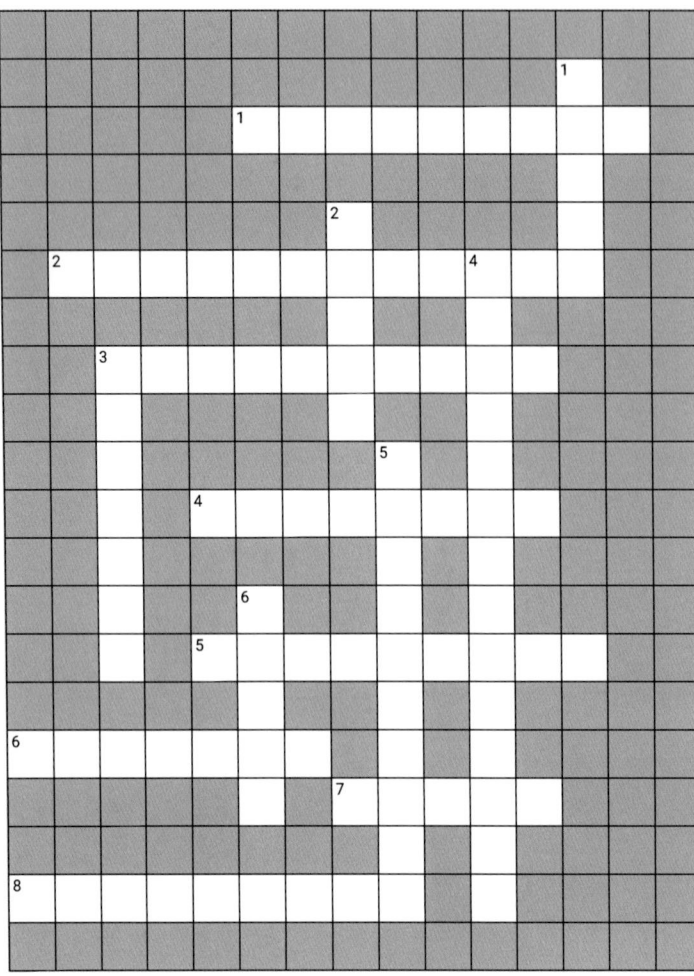

ACROSS
1. Dinosaurs
2. Caterpillars
3. Crocodiles
4. Dolphins
5. Hedgehogs
6. Beavers
7. Foxes
8. Elephants

DOWN
1. Frogs
2. Birds
3. Cougars
4. Apes and Monkeys
5. Chameleons
6. Bears

Puzzle 2

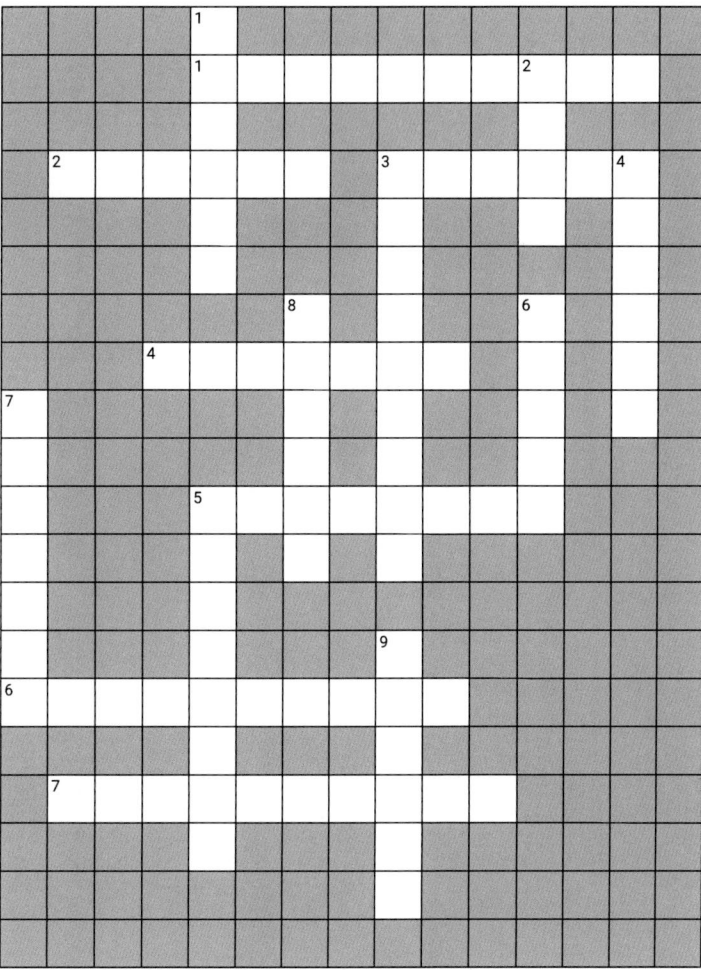

ACROSS
1. Alligators
2. Tigers
3. Koalas
4. Alpacas
5. Peacocks
6. Sea Turtles
7. Rhinoceros

DOWN
1. Camels
2. Owls
3. Kangaroos
4. Snakes
5. Penguins
6. Lions
7. Spiders
8. Pandas
9. Zebras

Puzzle 3

ACROSS
1. Meerkat
2. Lizards
3. Fish
4. Parrots
5. Hyena
6. Leopards
7. Iguanas
8. Gazelle
9. Insects

DOWN
1. Jellyfish
2. Jaguars
3. Ostriches
4. Octopuses
5. Bats
6. Flamingo
7. Moose
8. Lynx

Puzzle 4

ACROSS
1. Starfish
2. Whales
3. Ponies
4. Roosters
5. Anteater
6. Armadillo
7. Wolves
8. Scorpions

DOWN
1. Swans
2. Seahorses
3. Seals and Sea Lions
4. Pigs and Piglets
5. Polar Bears
6. Buffalo
7. Cows

Puzzle 5

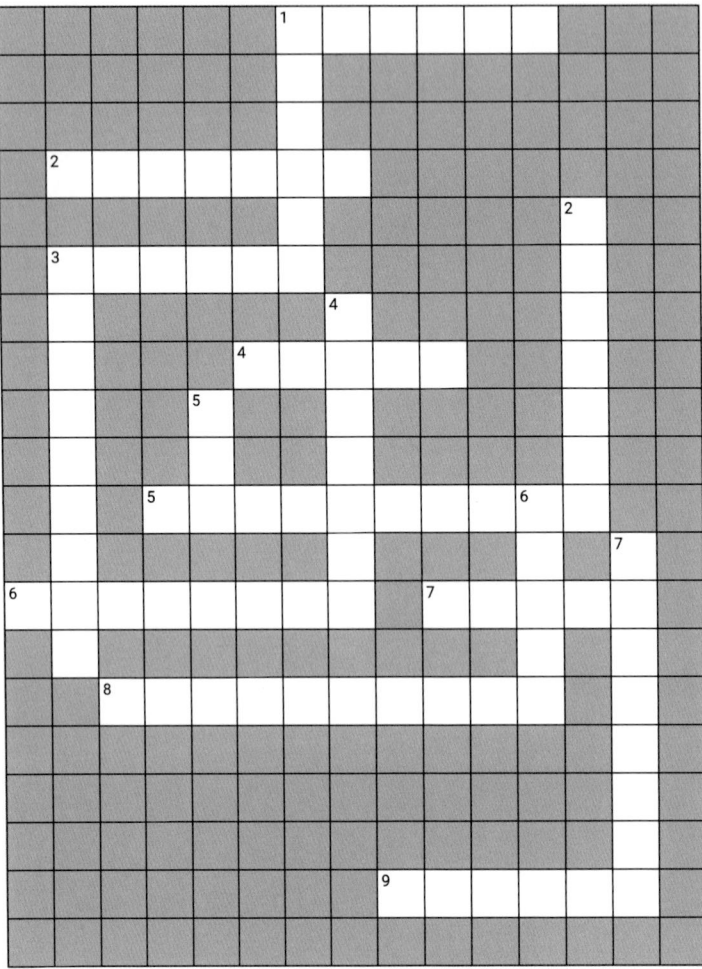

ACROSS
1. Sloths
2. Echidna
3. Storks
4. Sheep
5. Guinea Pigs
6. Platypus
7. Llama
8. Porcupines
9. Sharks

DOWN
1. Skunks
2. Donkeys
3. Squirrels
4. Ferrets
5. Emu
6. Goats
7. Raccoons

Puzzle 6

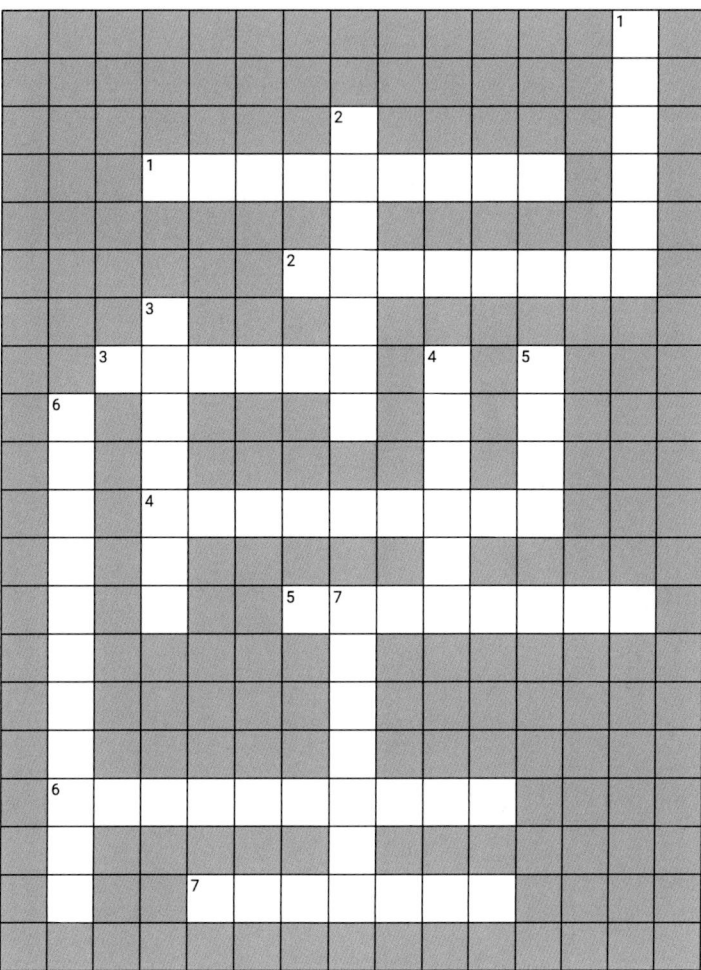

ACROSS
1. Tortoises
2. Gorillas
3. Cattle
4. Aardvarks
5. Opossums
6. Amphibians
7. Weasels

DOWN
1. Lemurs
2. Coyotes
3. Mammals
4. Walrus
5. Yaks
6. Farm Animals
7. Puffins

Puzzle 1

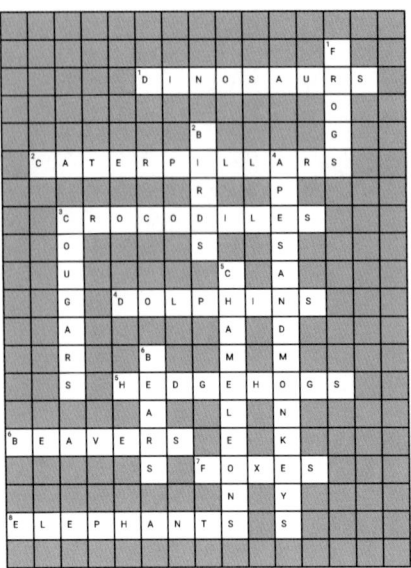

Puzzle 2

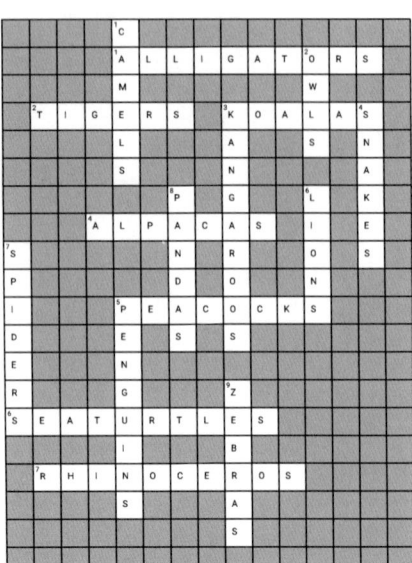

Puzzle 3

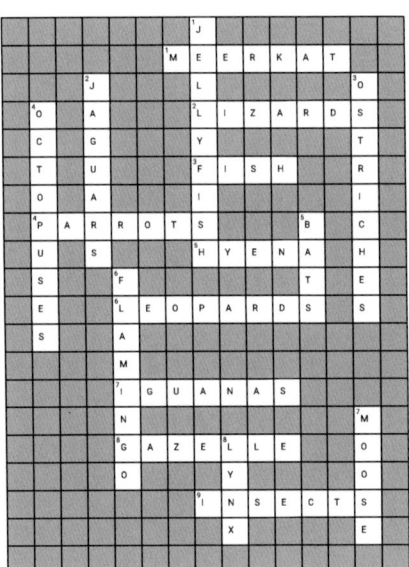

Puzzle 4

Puzzle 5

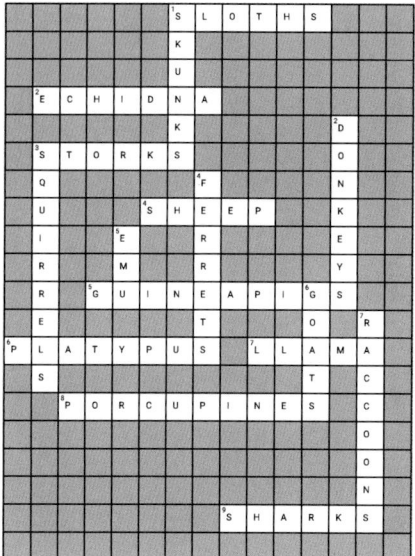

Puzzle 6

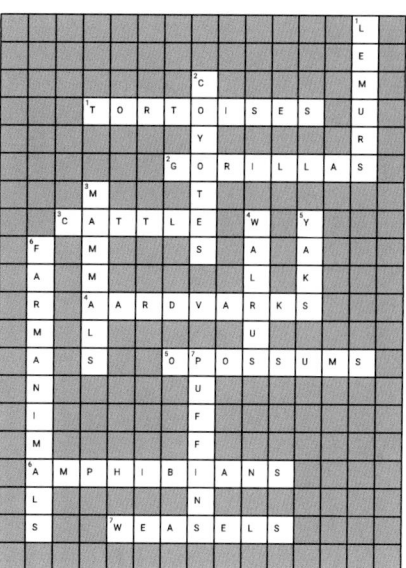

Made in the USA
Middletown, DE
19 June 2023

32832176R00020